Unopened Books

Multiplying the 2%

Jermaine D. Gassaway

ISBN: 1546985875
ISBN-13:9781546985877

DEDICATION

This book is dedicated to three very special women in my life. My mother the late Patricia A. Gassaway, my wonderful wife Apri Gassaway and daughter Abigail Gassaway. My mother taught me to dream, believe, and trust in my Lord and Savior. My wife is my best friend, life partner, and biggest supporter. She believed in me even when I did not believe in myself. She gave me the greatest gift one could ask for; my daughter, Abigail.

Unopened Books

CONTENTS

Unopened Books

ACKNOWLEDGMENTS

I would like to thank the many people who stood with me while writing this book; to those who encouraged me when doubt crept in, bounced ideas back and forth, read, contributed, or assisted in the editing, proofreading, and design.

A heartfelt thanks to my wife for being my biggest supporter and critic to ensure this book is an accurate reflection of my personal narrative and beliefs about education. I love you and appreciate your sacrifice more than you will ever know.

A special thanks to my mentor and father figure Tim "Coach" States, professional mentor Kimberly Bland, and my Uncle Jacob Major. Coach, thank you for being a wonderful friend and source of support and guidance over the many years. Mrs. Bland, thank you for coaching and pushing me to truly learn the skill of teaching and learning, and leadership. Uncle Jacob, thank you for guiding me down a path that allowed me to become the man that I am today.

Unopened Books

Introduction

> The impulse to dream was slowly beaten out of me by experience. Now it surged up again and I hungered for books, new ways of looking and seeing.
>
> —Richard Wright

One cold winter day in Detroit, Michigan, I shook the hands of two Black male students. At face value, nothing seemed peculiar about this gesture; I was a teacher, and it was the way that I greeted every student, every day, who walked through my classroom door. However, this particular interaction led me down a path that I normally do not travel. It made me consider whether that these two students were on two distinct trajectories.

At about 2 p.m. that school day, I was walking through the hallways of Detroit Edison Public School Academy, a K-12 network of public charter schools in Detroit, MI, to meet a kindergarten teacher whom I will call Ms. Brown. She stopped to ask me to take a Black male student to the office who had been misbehaving in class. I tend to ask myself in these situations, "what could a kindergartener possibly do to get himself kicked out of class?" Now, I am sure educators across the globe could answer that question; but for some strange reason I was unable to immediately respond to her in that moment. I thought to myself, "should I attempt to talk to the student or just ignore her request altogether and keep walking?" I also considered whether to take him to the office and let him get in trouble or handle the situation my way.

In a moment of radical honesty, I reluctantly chose to take the student with me and handle the situation my way. From the moment I looked him in the eye, shook his hand, and said to him, "come with me", this five-year-old kid's demeanor shifted. In fact, he immediately wanted to complete his schoolwork, and followed every directive given. It was clear once I was with the student that his behavior was not the primary issue. Of course, I gave him the typical "education is important", and "misbehaving in class will not be tolerated" speech. I talked to him about his behavior and the consequences associated with it. I elaborated about the importance of getting a quality education no matter who was in front of him, or who he liked or disliked. After a while, I took him back to class instead of taking him to the office. However, later that day, he got into a fight with another student and was immediately suspended from school.

As I pondered my actions and the actions of the kindergarten student; I asked myself: was he really on a downward trajectory or was he desperately longing for care, guidance, and support from an authoritative figure that he could relate to - maybe a Black male? Now, I am not suggesting that Black men have all the answers to resolve our education crisis here in America, but I know from firsthand experience that having a Black male teacher in the classroom gives added benefit to students, particularly if they are African American -- and more specifically, African American boys.

At the very same school, I shook the hand of a twelfth-grade student who had recently received several offers from prestigious colleges and universities around the country. I paused and thought to myself, "what is so different about this student that placed him on a path toward college?" Was it his determination? Was it his focus? Was it the fact that he came from a "better" background than the kindergarten student? No. No. And no! I later learned that a key difference in these two students was that the twelfth grader had a mentor in his life at an early age, who just so happened to be a Black male. Unaware of its significance, the twelfth grader spoke to me about the transformative opportunity to see someone who looked like him dream, set goals, achieve them, and pour into others. His mentor represented the man he sought to become. His body language captured the student's attention and his voice awakened his drive to succeed. An education became something he wanted and that he knew he could achieve.

Here you have two students attending the same K-12 school but at opposite ends of the spectrum. One may experience potentially unavoidable hardships, while the other is on a path to master the stages of life—all because one Black male took the time to pour into one Black boy.

The sad reality is that by the time students are in the third grade, prisons are being built on the basis of how many fail standardized tests or get wrapped up in America's juvenile justice system. For far too many students of color, the gateway to incarceration begins with a referral from the classroom to the courtroom. This phenomenon is referred to as the "school-to-prison pipeline." The NAACP Legal Defense Fund describes this pipeline as a "funneling of students out of school and into the streets and the juvenile correctional system." How can the future of a seven-year-old be based solely on a test score? And how can we change his trajectory? These are the questions that many educators, including myself, continue to grapple with. This is where my work begins.

As I was thinking about writing this book, I recalled a song by Kirk Franklin entitled "Smile." It has affected many people across the nation and could be the soundtrack for my twenty-eight years on Earth. This book revolves around the value, and significance of a smile. It is all about the life-changing person who can reach a kindergarten, first-, or twelfth-grade student and help them realize their potential in life. For me, this is my life's work. It is what wakes me up in the morning and motivates me when challenges arise. My dad died from lung cancer when I was fifteen years old. My mentor "Coach States", uncle, and a couple select teachers, all of whom were Black, stepped up to help me get through, and stay focused on my journey to college. All kids need the same community of support and covering. That is why I committed myself to education.

If it were solely up to me, I would refuse to allow our students to join the staggering number of Black Americans who become dropouts, prison inmates, illiterate adults, and early casualties. But I am just one person. We need more. We need Black males who are geared up and ready for war. We need more men who will fight in this educational army. But most importantly, we need more Black men who are prepared to just smile at our kids on a daily basis, at their sporting events and before, during, and after school activities. Although this may not seem like much, I have seen that smile alone bring many students to tears, provide inspiration, and cultivate them into math and literacy superstars.

We are in dire need of Black male educators to serve as models, not only for the Black community, but also for the community at large. Our kids need faces that mirror their own. They need people to look up to beyond athletes and rappers who are idolized on mainstream media outlets. We must counter the stereotype that Black Men are incapable of sustaining long-term job security or providing for their families. And, though many may see the added benefit of having Black male teachers, only a few truly understand the real challenges that they face in deciding to pursue a career in education.

When I was a fourth-grade teacher, I had a moment that shifted my understanding of the significance of Black male educators on the lives of children, especially young Black children. I was preparing to take my students outside after dismissal. Since it was cold, I wrapped my scarf around my neck; however, when I looked to my left, I saw several of my male students trying to imitate me. Bemused, I walked over and asked, "What are you guys doing?" They replied, "We're trying to be like you, Mr. Gassaway!" In that very moment, even in the seemingly trivial nature of the act, it dawned on me that our little Black boys and girls look to me as a role model, someone they could look up to, believe in, and model themselves after.

This was an eye opener. While I knew my students respected me, I had no idea that they paid such close attention to my every move. I then started paying closer attention to my students and their behaviors, and found countless other examples of similar interactions. It affirmed my thinking. There are significant benefits to have Black males in education. Now, let me be clear, I've worked with some pretty awesome non-Black, male and female teachers who have poured their hearts and lives into low-income students, and students of color. I admire and truly respect and value their work and commitment to all children. However, this book is geared toward encouraging Black males to get involved in education, whether through the doors of the classroom or through mentorship opportunities. It is geared toward awakening that smile for teachers, mentors, and kids. It is about changing the trajectory of the kindergartener. It is about meeting the needs of students with a smile that silently utters these words: "I understand."

Unopened Books

CHAPTER 1
So, What? I Don't Want to Be a Teacher.

> Every man must decide whether he will walk in the light of creative altruism or in the darkness of destructive selfishness.
>
> —Dr. Martin Luther King, Jr.

Imagine using a lighter to light a candle. The candle lights the room, which lights the house, which can be seen from miles away. In that same regard, one person can teach or mentor a young boy or girl, who will grow up to teach or mentor someone else.

Most parents remember the jaw-dropping experience of witnessing their child begin to walk. For my wife and me, this event was somewhat anticipated, but still came at a special time. My daughter Abigail took her first surreal nine steps on my wife's first Mother's Day. For us, it was the most exciting thing that could have ever happened. However, we started teaching and preparing our daughter months before she actually started walking.

Our kids in underserved communities deserve the same kind of preparation from caring and informed teachers and mentors. I hear the phrase, "I don't want to be a teacher," over and over. Believe me, I get it. Some of you may have hesitated to pick up this book simply because you know that this is not your calling. To you, I say, you may be right. But your presence is still needed in some form, whether in the classroom or on the playground.

Although teaching full time is a vocation, when we consider how the word is defined, we can begin to understand that we are all teachers. Yes, even you. Think about the last time you showed someone how to do something, whether it was teaching a niece or a nephew how to tie his or her shoes, or perhaps helping a first grader learn how to read. This is teaching in its purest form. Just admit it: we are all walking, talking, breathing teachers. Granted, when you place twenty-five to thirty students in one classroom, it changes the dynamics of the situation; however, it does not make you more or less of a teacher. Teaching requires a different skill set than most professions, and although it is undervalued in many ways, it is essential to our communities and our nation.

Teachers make up the very fabric of American society; it is because of them that other professions exist. And even before people did it as a formal job, someone had to teach. Someone had to show nations of children, who looked like you and me, how to complete the simplest of tasks. More than just instructing us intellectually, someone had to mold us into young men and women. Consider this: Where would you be without your most life-changing teacher or mentor? Can you honestly say you would be where you are today? Most of us would acknowledge that we wouldn't.

Teachers and mentors are crucial because they represent a cultural exchange of experiences; they also profoundly affect the lives of those who have yet to venture into the world alone. Through conversation, relationships are forged and stories are told. This is where the trajectory changes for most kids and why the greatest thing you can give them is your time.

If we were to look back on our own K–12 educational experience, would we recall diversity being reflected in our teachers or in our classmates? The American school system is predominantly White. With the increasing influx of mixed races and minorities, our classrooms are beginning to resemble unidentified mirrors. The idea is simple. In an unidentified mirror, you can see yourself; however, you are unable to see the reflection that mirrors your likeness, which is the teacher or the mentor.

Did you know that only 2% of all teachers are Black males?[1] This statistic is downright unfathomable. How can a population of men be destined for prison rather than for educational institutions? How can a jail cell be a better mirror of their lives than a college campus? All across America, students of color are experiencing these same trends within their neighborhoods. How do we change the future of the young Black men and women of our era? It is simple. We teach. We mentor.

For the 2% of Black men in the educational sector, their reach is minimal, at best. However, teaching should never be confined to a space; it should adapt to meet the needs of the ones being taught. Think about it. As a coach, you teach. So why do we, as adults, limit teaching to a space rather than define it as a way we have evolved to transfer ideas from one person to the next? The reason may be because we see it as a profession, rather than as a skill that we can alter to suit the setting. Only when we begin to view the word "teacher" differently will more of us become effective educators.

---

[1] Valerie Strauss, "Black male teachers: There aren't enough of them," *Washington Post,* 28 Apr. 2015, 2 Feb. 2017, <https://www.washingtonpost.com/news/answer-sheet/wp/2015/04/28/black-male-teachers-there-arent-enough-of-them/>

We need one another to fill in the gaps—the gaps that cannot be filled within a six- to seven-hour school day. We need you, teacher. Perhaps you are saying, "I don't know where to start." My answer is to get involved. Volunteer. Show up at your neighborhood school. Demand your place in education as a Black male. When our students see us, they see themselves. Help them connect the fragments of their existence by being a presence in your local school. Your role does not have to be in the classroom. You can mentor a group of young men, or allow students to shadow you once a week at your place of employment. It is this type of connection that bridges the gap between generations and communities.

Be the voice. Be the change. Be the teacher.

Unopened Books

CHAPTER 2
Historical Context: The Plight of Education

> Taking tests is stressful, but bubbling in a Scantron does not stop bullets from bursting. I hear education systems are failing, but I believe they're succeeding at what they're built to do—to train you, to keep you on track, to track down an American dream that has failed so many of us all.
>
> —Malcolm London

You have a voice, right? According to the *Merriam-Webster Dictionary*, to "voice" means *to give utterance or expression to, to declare, or to proclaim, whether in written or verbal form.* In this chapter, I want to illustrate the plight of education and the pressing need for more Black men to use their voice in education.

No nation is perfect, and as a country, we fall far short of the mark in far too many fields. However, education is one of the worst. The rollercoaster of education policies and our subpar efforts to raise standards are merely masks that hide, rather than fix, our growing problems. The history of education in America consists of a series of similar policies that we have continued to adopt despite their manifested failure. Our education system is like a puzzle; lawmakers, business leaders, and district overseers keep inserting pieces that were not meant to fit. Although some may agree with the idea that education can be run as a business, to those within the field, this concept seems illogical. Teachers often ask, "How can a business leader, who has never set foot in a classroom, tell me what is best when he sees students merely as statistics?" The truth is that he can't. Experience tells us that you must be a part of the system to change the system; only in education is this not deemed to be true. To make it plain, why do we continue to allow politicians and individuals with the deepest pockets - many of whom have never taught or stepped in a school for that matter - to set policies and regulations about how to educate all children; in particular, Black males.

Education in America can be traced as far back as the Colonial era in 1647, when it was used as a means to uphold religious faith. The Puritans wanted to ensure that their children adhered to sound religious doctrines and could effectively spread them to others. It was not until

1779, under the leadership of President Thomas Jefferson, that schooling became more formalized. Jefferson sought to establish a two-track education system for "the laboring and the learned." The idea of the two-track system is still prevalent today; however, it is more visible in certain districts than in others.

I can remember someone sharing his high school experience in 2010 and noting the two-track system within South Carolina schools. One track was for those who were headed for educational success, and the other was for those who were not "quite" at grade level. I believe that some students were sent "up the road" to receive a better education, while those who were failing were left to fail miserably. The tracking system within America became a widely debated issue about ten years ago; now, we have a new "pathway" system that divides students into "college prep" or "technical." The classes students take depend on their test scores and grades. The idea is the same, but the terms are different. We can continue to change the language, but it will never justify the system.

In 1785, the Continental Congress passed a law that authorized the creation of townships, each of which had to allot a percentage of land to a local school. Initially, a free public education was granted only to poor children, while rich families had to pay. However, in 1827, Massachusetts extended this right to all students, regardless of their financial status. Although during this era, the American education system tried to level the playing field, non-Whites were not afforded the same opportunities. As a result of the period's racial climate, populations were still ostracized, even when they were at last permitted to receive an education. Indeed, education was a tool that was used to limit communication; legislators opined that if a man was unable to articulate what he desired in either verbal or written form, he would never be able to access it. Education was a means of stripping people of their cultural identity in an attempt to establish the culture, beliefs, and ideas of the majority. For instance, in 1864, Congress made it illegal for Native Americans to be taught in their own languages. The government sent Native American children to boarding schools, whose goal, as one Bureau of Indian Affairs official put it, was to "kill the Indian and save the man."

This same idea persists in our public schools, as the identities of minorities continue to be misplaced. We have allowed America to use education as a vehicle of cultural capital. Indeed, Pierre Bourdieu suggests that "the educational system of industrialized societies functions in such a way as to legitimate class inequalities." Essentially, the knowledge and culture of the higher class are infused within our education system. Thus, to succeed, students must speak the language of this group. For example, the word "yacht" is most relevant to the higher class, and if it were to be put on a test, a student from a low-income background would have a significant disadvantage. Such examples reinforce the data suggesting that Caucasian students are surpassing their minority counterparts in academia, and until the inequalities of language and culture are eliminated, we cannot view education as entirely equal. The reality is that we need mirrors within the education field that can serve as a role model for students and enhance their understanding of the world through their own cultural lens, and this is where the Black male mentor or educator comes into play.

It was not until 1865, at the end of the Civil War, that legislators called Blacks to bring education to the South. However, although they were ostensibly granted the same access as their White counterparts to a free public education, in practice, their opportunities were much fewer. In relation to the establishment of schools, Blacks controlled the South, but during the Reconstruction era in 1893, Whites regained political power, laying the foundations of legal segregation. The 1896 case, *Plessy v. Ferguson,* reinforced the idea of "separate but equal." This case justified racial segregation in all areas, including public schools. Nearly sixty years later, the Supreme Court unanimously agreed that separate schools were "inherently unequal" in the landmark case, *Brown v. Board of Education of Topeka*. Although this decision unbarred the doors of segregation, efforts toward inclusion would be met with brutal force and indifference. Moreover, while America no longer had nominally separate school systems, geographical rezoning and redistricting were still permitted. In *Milliken v. Bradley* in 1974, the Supreme Court, under the leadership of President Richard Nixon, reinforced the *Brown v. Board* decision; however, it legally sanctioned putting students of color in inner-city districts and placing Caucasian students in wealthier, predominantly White suburbs.

The same issues that were present decades ago still exist within our schools, and their impact is even greater now than it was previously. In 1893, school boards transitioned from being run by community leaders and local small business owners, to being governed by doctors, lawyers, big businessmen, and members of the highest class. As policies began to change, the idea of the "one size fits all" model emerged; districts adopted the same instructional practices to meet the needs of different students from diverse populations. So, how can a system be crafted for all without failing to meet the needs of some for the sake of the whole? It cannot. This helicopter approach to education also gives rise to the "savior complex," which suggests that if the needed resources are dumped into communities, inequalities will magically disappear. Not so. If we continue to fly overhead, dumping resources into communities, but never touch down to provide authentic and targeted support we will continue to waste valuable tax dollars in the name of education.

Districts across America are different. Some schools have the latest technology, while others have outdated curriculum materials, broken desks, and unfit conditions. If you do not believe me, travel to the rural counties along I-95 in South Carolina to witness what has been termed the "Corridor of Shame." Video footage shows roofs that are collapsing and school buildings that are inadequately furnished. Students should never have to worry about mold or decaying infrastructure. How can we expect them to learn if the environment in which they are placed is not conducive to a quality education?

The history of education in America has been one of both triumph and defeat. Due to our nation's racial encapsulation, schooling has continued to be segregated in both practice and theory. According to the 2014 School Discipline Report of the U.S. Department of Education Office for Civil Rights, Black children represented 18% of preschool enrollment; however, 48% of this population received more than one out-of-school suspension. By contrast, White students represented 43% of preschool enrollment; however, only 26% of them were suspended more than once. On average, Black students are three times more likely to be suspended or expelled in comparison to their White counterparts.[2]

The statistics are startling, and I could go on and on about the problems that exist within education. But listing the problems does nothing if I am not advocating for solutions. America is in need of teachers like you and me: those who have been called to the classroom and those who have been called to mentor or to support education through the use of their voice. Education will never change until we change how we define the term "teacher." Within each of us lies a teacher, and it is our responsibility, for the sake of our kids, to articulate what they are unable to.

My intent in this chapter was not to be negative in my analysis of how race interacts with the education system; however, the facts are the facts. Moreso, my intent was to emphasize why the role of the Black male teacher is so important. How long will we allow our Black men and women to be sidelined by a system that is hidden in plain sight? How long will we remain mute on the issues of educational reform? How long will we allow our silence to be our stance? How long are we truly willing to wait? For me, I can wait no longer.

---

[2] *Center for Public Education,* National School Boards Association, 2017, 2 Feb., 2017 <www.centerforpubliceducation.org>

CHAPTER 3
Turning Pages: Be the Voice

People pay for what they do, and still for what they have allowed themselves to become. And they pay for it very simply; by the lives they lead.

—James Baldwin

One might call me strange to think that I would make a comparison between our students and books. However, this is my intent. We need more Black male voices, more men who are not afraid to join the dialogue happening all around the world. As I reflect on Black males like Geoffrey Canada, Cornell West, Paul Hill, Dr. Steve Perry, Freeman Hrabowski, Dr. Pedro Noguera, and Ralph Bland, to name a few, who are revolutionizing educational opportunities for kids across this nation, I am left wondering: where are the other voices?

Education and books are directly related. When you think about a book, what comes to mind? I would suggest its ability to provide information. You might tell me what genre of literature you prefer, such as suspense, drama, or romance novels. The formal definition of a book is "a handwritten or printed work of fiction or nonfiction, usually on sheets of paper fastened or bound together within covers."

If you open a book, you are given a wealth of knowledge. In that regard, our kids are books, too. They come to us filled with information. They're filled with interesting facts, passions, and insights. However, if our books remain closed or are never opened, they become dust collectors, cup coasters, or space wasters on our bookshelves. Similarly, if we never unlock our kids' potential or peel the pages, we can never impart information or learn from them. What I am stating here is simple. It's our job as educators to help our kids open up, so we can first learn from them and then teach them. Fundamentally, it's about building relationships. I have seen too many teachers stand in front of kids, never introducing themselves or taking the time to learn their names. As educators, we must recognize that our kids are real and should be treated as such. Throughout my career in education, I have grown so much from my students, and it started with me first getting to know them.

This truth is even more devastating for our young people. Just think about it. If you never had someone open a book and read it to you, what would have happened? Imagine someone who never learned to read because he or she did not have access to books growing up. How deadly would it be? Essentially, this person would roam the earth in an unconscious state.

The power and liberation that we find in books are priceless. If we do not open our books, they will continue to become the growing number of Black men that occupy our prisons; they will become the people who perpetuate the cycle of poverty, and ultimately, who become statistics and not examples. They will become the tax takers rather than the tax makers. Essentially, they will become the problem. All because we allowed the books in our lives to collect dust, promising that one day, we would read them. But the phrase, "one day," implies a distant future. How long are we, as a people, willing to wait? As educators, we can wait no longer. We must crack our books open. We must help our students navigate each paragraph and color the pictures. We must be there for them as they turn the page. If we spark their interest, cultivate their curiosity, and teach them to exceed expectations, they will be able to write their own pages. Those pages will turn into chapters, and ultimately, into a book that was designed and edited by them. Their book will be written once they take what they have learned and given it back to others who can relate to their journey.

We all have certain genres that we find pleasure in reading. According to the National Center for Education Statistics, in the fall of 2012, approximately 51% of the students in public schools were White, and 49% were minorities. In the fall of 2024, it is projected that the number of White students will decrease to 46%, and the number of minorities will increase to 54% in public schools.[3] The changing dynamics in American society speak to why I consider our kids to be books that must be read by a more diverse education workforce. They need readers not only like me, but like you, too. Together, we can offer them a set of unique perspectives and experiences that will help expose them to their culture and history. However, the current education system does not reflect this need for ethnic diversity. If only 2% of our teachers are Black men, our kids are not benefiting from the "cultural capital" of this group, not just in low-income areas, but in affluent areas as well. Black men are needed in every school, every day, whether in traditional or nontraditional classroom settings.

As a reader, and as someone who has helped to turn

[3] National Center for Education Statistics, "Racial/Ethnic Enrollment in Public Schools," *NCES Website,* May 2016, 2 Feb. 2017 <http://nces.ed.gov/programs/coe/indicator_cge.asp>

the pages of so many unopened books, I know how privileged I would feel to have a reader that was similar to me. Again, in no way am I suggesting that only Black males can turn our kids' pages. But time and time again, I get appreciation letters that confirm, in some regard, that I am a commodity in the education field. I have worked at several schools and sat on numerous committees in which I have been one of the only Black male educators present. If we are ever going to resolve the civil rights issues of our time, we must start by diversifying our workforce - starting with Black male educators.

I'm writing about the real needs that exist, and how we can all do something about them. We need more Black men in the education field and in leadership roles, participating at the decision-making table, discussing policies that will affect the books that sit, eagerly awaiting someone to read them. After all, an unopened book will never be able to turn its own pages.

Again, I ask: where are the other voices? I can share my perspective at the decision-making table, but if there is no one there to validate my experiences, who reflects my existence, I am merely a voice in a crowd. One man cannot do it alone; it takes people like you and me, who are willing to use our voices to change the trajectory of our young men and women within our communities. These young men and women deserve a fighting chance to unleash the greatness within them. But if no one ever speaks for them, they will forever be accounted for by our silence.

CHAPTER 4
Poverty Is a State of Mind

Anyone who has ever struggled with poverty knows how extremely expensive it is to be poor.

—James Baldwin

Christopher Gardner:	Hey. Don't ever let somebody tell you ... you can't do something. Not even me. All right?
Christopher [son]:	All right.
Christopher Gardner:	You got a dream...you gotta protect it. People can't do somethin' themselves, they wanna tell you—you can't do it. If you want something, go get it. Period.

In the movie, *The Pursuit of Happyness*, Will Smith plays a struggling homeless salesman trying to care for his five-year-old son. He is on the verge of a life-altering career change from an intern to a stockbroker. Based on the real life of Chris Gardner, the film speaks volumes about the protagonist's character and integrity. The movie version of Gardner chases a guy for stealing his time machine; in a cab, he puts together a Rubik's Cube in a matter of minutes; he almost misses an interview because he is arrested for unpaid parking tickets; he runs miles to the interview location covered in paint; he and his son are thrown out of their motel; and he is then forced to sleep on the bathroom floor of a subway station. Tears drop from his face as he tries to keep his son from waking up when an unknown person is trying to force their way in.

There is one scene that resonates with me the most, and, I would guess, with many others in the education field: the basketball scene. Honestly, if you have not watched the movie, I encourage you to do so. In this scene, Chris and his five-year-old son Christopher are playing basketball together. Chris says to his son, "You will probably be as good as I was, and I was below average; so, you will probably rank somewhere around there so I don't want you shooting this ball around all day and night." At this point, Christopher gets upset and throws the ball down. This is when Chris stops and says, "Don't you ever let someone tell you—you can't do something, not even me. You got a dream; you gotta protect it. If you want something, go get it. Period."

Jermaine Gassaway, an unopened book, was once a poor Black boy who wishes he'd had someone tell him at the age of five to never give up on his dreams. As a native of Washington, D.C., I am the youngest of five children born to the late Patricia Gassaway and the late James Earl Major, Sr. Now, I must admit, my mom did everything in her power to ensure that I had what I needed. She worked the midnight shift at the local Texaco gas station on the southwest side of town. She did the best she could, given her circumstances, but I vividly remember sneaking to the neighbor's house to steal water from the outside faucet to fill about twenty- two liter bottles so I could wash up and flush the toilet when the water was turned off. This happened several times. I remember lighting candles to see in the house at night and to complete homework assignments. I remember sleeping on the couch with a coat in the middle of December because the heat had been turned off. Or seeing the holes in plastic bags from rats in our house. Or pumping gas at the local gas station in D.C., just to make money so I could buy food. The blessing in this story is that I always knew that I was destined for something greater. But not all kids have that inner voice or believe it even if they do.

I personally believe that it was the gift I received from my grandmother—the gift of sharing her faith about the Lord Jesus Christ—that had one of the greatest impacts on my life. She taught me how to pray, and the importance of prayer. As an eight-year-old kid, I was the only person in my household of three brothers and one sister to have the church van pick me up to attend Sunday School and worship service. This, to me, was the start of my transformation. Church was just like the basketball clip in *The Pursuit of Happyness*. It is where I learned to never give up on my goals, no matter what. Now, at that age, I didn't realize the importance of going to church, but I went to make my grandmother happy. Little did I know that its impact would be incomprehensible. It is the reason that I am here today. My grandmother saved me when I made some bad decisions. My past as a child does not have to define me but it does inform my views on life and my call to influence the lives of children. It's just a state of mind. I thank my grandmother, the late Jannie Robinson, for motivating me to know the Lord for myself and for encouraging me to be saved at the age of sixteen. As a young man, I experienced a lot, but walked away with something greater: my Lord and Savior Jesus Christ and the belief that I, too, have the gift of choice.

I shared that part of my personal narrative to illustrate the similarities between my life story and the life stories of so many students whom educators stand in front of every day.

It is a narrative that is all too common in schools across the nation. It is our moral, societal responsibility to peel back the pages of all students, particularly students coming from the harshest circumstances. Students arrive at our doors with layers of armor on - bullet proof vests, knee pads, shoulder pads, helmets, fatigues, combat boots, brass knuckles - to survive a myriad of difficult circumstances. This armor is used to protect them from physical or emotional abuse, neighborhood or community level violence, hunger, family instability and other factors that force kids to protect themselves by any means necessary. There is a tremendous amount of effort required to read the pages of each book, but imagine how more knowledgeable one might become if they just took the time. You might realize that "Demetris", for example, walks the long way to school to avoid run ins with shady suspects but on the way to school passes a small graveyard that has captured his curiosity and interest in the idea of mortuary science.

In *A Framework for Understanding Poverty,* Dr. Ruby K. Payne gives us a working definition: "Poverty is the extent to which an individual does without resources. Those resources could be financial, emotional, mental, spiritual, and physical, which are not limited to: support systems, relationships/role models, and knowledge of hidden rules." Now, I am aware that low-income families or families in urban communities do not necessarily fit this definition.

But there are aspects of poverty that families, or people, in any social group may face. I am suggesting that certain resources, specifically emotional support systems and role models, are not readily accessible to kids in low-income communities. I've witnessed this both personally and professionally. While poverty is a state of mind, it is also a daunting truth that children face daily. They can live in single-family households with limited to no support, whether at school or at home. I know it is impossible to save every child, every day, but the point is that kids do not have the support to look beyond their circumstances or communities to see a different way of life. It is as if planes are flying overhead dropping in resources, but the resources are being distributed ineffectively due to a lack of oversight and direction. Thus, kids don't have a guided pathway to achieve their dreams because its not been clearly defined.

In some schools, there are few people who look like the kids I'm describing. The only ones who resemble them are their classmates. If you were to take a nationwide survey, you would notice that Black male educators are clustered primarily in at-risk schools; thus, they usually serve in disciplinary roles. Black male teachers are needed across this country, not just in high-need areas. Diversity benefits all and cultivates innovation. Our kids need emotional resources to cope with their often difficult circumstances. This is what is missing in education. Our schools are filled with individuals. But when Black male students walk those halls and look over their shoulders, no one is really there who looks like them. They are left searching for someone who will address their insecurities and reaffirm their identity.

The Black male is missing.

Our young male students often do not get a chance to see a reflection of themselves. And our young female students may not get to see how Black men engage with them on a daily basis. Black males do not witness their likeness when they enter the doors of our schools. Why? Because there is a gap in education that keeps our kids in poverty because of the barriers associated with the absence of the Black male.

Black men face many obstacles that affect their decision to enter and stay in education. Five of these barriers are: (1) lack of respect within the field; (2) lack of career advancement; (3) diminution of financial sustainability; (4) typecasting into disciplinary roles; and (5) demanding workloads. I will dive a little deeper into these five barriers to unpack a little later on in the book, but they are real issues for Black men, and consequently, for our kids in our neighborhood school systems.

Unopened Books

CHAPTER 5
The Need

The world cares very little about what a man or woman knows; it is what a man or woman is able to do that counts.

—Booker T. Washington

Dr. Martin Luther King, Jr. was a man of great faith and great intellect. Dr. King's position on education was more than asking that students memorize the Pythagorean Theorem ($a^2+b^2 = c^2$) or the Fisher effect. He was more concerned about the holistic development of humanity. As educators, this is our goal. Anyone can recall historic events, social concepts, or locations on a map, but what purpose does this serve outside of a test? None. Our mission should be to develop productive, educated citizens who think intensively within the parameters of their moral compass. That's powerful. I don't teach just so kids can pass a standardized assessment. Although this may be vital to their long-term success, it should not nor has to be the primary goal for educators.

In *The New Jim Crow*, Michelle Alexander, a civil rights lawyer and legal scholar, writes about the redesign of the racial caste system in America. Alexander talks specifically about mass incarceration and how the criminal justice system functions as a contemporary system of racial control. Alexander also notes that in Washington, D.C., our nation's capital, it is estimated that three out of every four young Black men (and nearly all of those in the poorest neighborhoods) can expect to serve time in prison; in my case, it was three out of four—I was the one who never had to go. As a DC native, I have seen the invasive presence of the judicial system within ethnic communities, and its corrosive effects on Black males, Black families, and Black neighborhoods.

By teaching the whole person, we, as educational activists, can utilize our talents to shape our students into innovative, creative, and self-sufficient citizens. Far too often in education, the conversation is solely about the data on academic and behavioral performance. Rarely do we discuss the socio-emotional needs of kids in low-income communities, especially those who lack a Black male influence. School principals, political leaders, law enforcement officers, parents/guardians, and other community-based groups would benefit greatly from a radicalized learning experience that re-educates those in power how to nurture and educate the whole child. In turn, this would allow our young people to acquire the skills to become future community leaders and advocates for the world. One might argue that our kids can't go very far without the necessary academic abilities to pass college admission assessments; critics would suggest that as ethnic communities, we should concentrate on the academic side of education. Well, if you don't know, let me tell you: you can't teach a kid who is more concerned about finding his or her next meal, or preparing for their walk home. Malcolm London, a poet from Chicago, powerfully articulates the state of education in his district. In his poem, "High School Training Grounds," he defines schools as being "diverse and segregated on purpose." London goes on to suggest that while "homework is our work," "bubbling Scantrons does not stop a bullet." Students enter the classroom weighed down by the argument that happened last night or the financial crisis that happened last month. Thus, as teachers and mentors, we must be conscious of the life experiences of our students. This is why the Black male is so pivotal in education. We need men who can identify with the struggles of our students, who can provide hope by merely sharing their experiences and consistently saying, "I understand." This type of sharing shows our kids that they, too, can overcome any situation. But if mentors or teachers never take the time, we will never really see behind our students' masks.

All too often, we, as educators, forget the human existence of our students. We forget the realities of their world, and we expect them to forget them, too. But if we look at our own lives, we can recognize that this mental model is unrealistic. This notion invalidates our students, causing us to see them as *tabulae rasae* or blank slates rather than as products of their lived experiences. We must understand that we are not our students, and our students are not us. Some students are so far removed from their education because of everything else happening in their lives. They learn to navigate the world based on what they have seen, which, in far too many cases, is an extremely limited view of what is possible.

The data over the past ten years suggests that our kids, black kids, are failing to make progress. This should be an utterly clear indication that their battle is not within the classroom, but outside of the four walls that are intended to shield them from their challenged reality. Don't believe me? Take another look at our prison system. As a society, we may be able to ignore that this is our truth. But we cannot ignore the implications of race in the classroom. Race matters. In fact, incarceration rates disproportionately favor men of color. One in every fifteen Black men is incarcerated in comparison to one in every 116 White men. According to the Bureau of Justice Statistics, one in three Black men can expect to go to prison in their lifetime. In addition, according to the National Association for the

Advancement of Colored People (NAACP), 35% of Black children in grades seven to twelve have been suspended or expelled at some point in their educational career compared to 15% of Whites. This is the reality for our young Black boys.

We often forget about the statement above: One in three Black men are expected to go to prison in their lifetime. However, this statement has always stuck with me. It has been a part of what I have witnessed all too often growing up in the inner city of Washington, D.C., with my three older brothers, all of whom were in prison during their teenage years. As the youngest, it was almost expected for me to follow them. Was it their fault that they sold drugs, and connected to the streets in order to get the bare essentials for them to eat, clothe themselves, or have money for metro fare? Some would say it was not. Though this narrative may resemble the stories of many young Black men growing up in low-income communities across this nation, it does not have to be this way. My brothers were just like me, smart, capable, and filled with potential to author the pages of their unopened books. The only difference was that I had an uncle and a mentor who invested time in me and rewarded me for making positive choices, like getting cash for good grades. Choice. An act of selecting or making a decision when faced with two or more possibilities. This is a difficult concept to teach a child who believes that having a choice does not apply to them.

Growing up, all my teachers were female, except for two Black men in my elementary school, one of whom held the more typical position for Black men in education, the physical education teacher. Nonetheless, my older brothers were my teachers. They taught me some of the most valuable lessons in my life, and it didn't require a syllabus or data-driven instruction. In fact, my oldest brother, who in my opinion is one of the smartest men I know academically, didn't allow me to hang on the corner to get involved in illegal activity, or hang out in the streets with them. He forced me to do more productive things with my time. We literally used to fight because I so badly wanted to participate in the activities they were involved in. But I'm more grateful than ever to him for sparing me unnecessary hard times. It allowed me to focus on other activities, like sports, which gave me an opportunity to practice the gift of choice.

Now, let's be clear, every Black male from a low-income community does not come from this kind of background. However, I am suggesting that for our most vulnerable populations to our more stable ones, there is a lack of influential Black men in our communities, and we can all benefit from changing that truth. For the first half of my life, the only males I knew were my brothers, uncle, second-grade teacher, and our White landlord. My mother did everything in her power to raise respectable, honorable men, but somewhere along the line, our height and testosterone got in the way. Before the start of every school year, I remember my mother scraping all of the money she had to buy school clothes, school supplies, and ensure our medical records were up-to-date. She tried her best to come to parent-teacher conferences. It was like the spirit of God kept telling me to hang on and get my education. Something kept saying that my current predicament was a mere test of faith and character, such that I would be placed in a unique position to help millions of students every day. This is what I leaned on to persevere. This is also why I continue to extend to others what was graciously extended to me. I remember telling my mom, "Someday I am going to call your job and tell you that it's your last day to work. You can let your boss know that your youngest son is here to take care of you. I want to return the time, energy, and resources you have poured into me."

For my brothers, the spirit of perseverance may have existed, but it didn't manifest itself in excelling in school. With the exception of my oldest brother, none of them completed high school, or stayed engaged in school beyond the ninth grade. My oldest brother received his General Educational Development (GED) diploma while he was at what used to be called Oak Hill Juvenile Detention Center in Laurel, Maryland. In fact, he had one of the highest scores the center had ever seen. I told you he was smart. As much as my mother hated the actions that led my brothers to end up in prison, we would wake up on Saturday mornings to ride a charter bus to this facility, filled with other Black mothers visiting their sons, to keep my brother encouraged and hopeful for better days to come. All three of my brothers fell victim to this place at one time or another during their childhood. These are the hard facts. Here you have four Black boys being raised in the inner city of Washington, DC. All four had the same opportunity to graduate from high school and move on to attend college; however, only one did. One out of four.

This is the statistic that I am tired of seeing. This is the statistic that I am tired of being connected to, either because of my personal background or simply being a Black man. I know as a nation; we can do better. Fannie Lou Hanner, a civil rights leader and philanthropist, once said: “I am sick and tired of being sick and tired.” These are my sentiments exactly. I am not suggesting that I am better than my brothers because I am most certainly not. Instead, I owe them so much and is what fuels me to change this narrative for Black kids. Why do we keep allowing our future leaders to be robbed of their education and wellbeing? Most say it is the right of every American to receive a quality education. But how many people really believe that? As a nation, if something doesn’t affect us personally, why get involved, right? No! This affects us all. For some, the impact may not be as immediate, but for others, the loss of a generation of Black males and females, sons and daughters, sisters and brothers weighs heavily on their shoulders each and every day. This is why I decided to become a teacher, school leader, soldier for good.

Over the years, I have watched my brothers, friends, and classmates struggle to develop the basic reading, writing, math, and soft skills necessary for success. One day, I was having a conversation with a few successful Black men from more affluent backgrounds, and they shared something that rubbed me the wrong way. They said, "I really want to help, but I often feel like an outsider." I exclaimed in confusion and a bit of frustration, “An outsider?” In an effort to explain, I pointed them to an excerpt from Dr. Martin Luther King Jr.’s “Letter from Birmingham Jail,” in which he had been incarcerated for eight days and where some called him an outsider:

> I think I should give the reason for my being in Birmingham since you have been influenced by the argument of "outsiders coming in."

> I am in Birmingham because injustice is here.... I am cognizant of the interrelatedness of all communities and states. I cannot sit idly by in Atlanta, and not be concerned about what happens in Birmingham. Injustice anywhere is a threat to justice everywhere. We are caught in an inescapable network of mutuality, tied in a single garment of

> destiny. Whatever affects one directly affects all indirectly. Never again can we afford to live with the narrow, provincial "outside agitator" idea. Anyone who lives inside the United States can never be considered an outsider.

Dr. King wrote this letter in response to a public statement of concern and caution issued by eight White religious leaders of the South. I agree with him. This "outsider mentality" of Black men, which stems from their fear of getting involved in the educational plight of our kids, is unacceptable. Anything that threatens the youth of this nation is "a threat to justice everywhere." We, as Black men, need to be the ones that infiltrate the school system to ensure that our kids have role models, images of themselves, and male guidance to reaffirm their identities in a world that has often displaced them. While the goal is to recruit and retain more Black men in education as both mentors and teachers, we must remember that we are all teachers; thus, the art of teaching is not limited to a building, but encompasses a community of like-minded individuals striving for equity within our neighborhood schools.

Throughout my K–12 education, I saw my peers get suspended and expelled at astronomical rates. They were missing valuable instructional time and compromising their dreams and aspirations. According to the Albert Shanker Institute, a nonprofit educational think tank, having more teachers of color in the classroom could alleviate the disproportionately high suspension rates for Black students. It is not just about keeping our kids from getting kicked out of school, but offering them an image of themselves while at school. It is about Black male educators and mentors building and maintaining a rapport with students and families. I have had many female teachers who were great instructionally, but could not pour into me what a male figure could. The reality is two-thirds of Black children live in single-parent households[4], and the vast majority are likely led by women. This poses a difficult task for anyone raising Black males, but especially women. The blessing, for me, was that I had older brothers, an influential uncle, and mentor who taught me the lessons that my mom could not. But not every child is afforded that. I often ask myself, where would I have ended up if it were not for the Black men in my life? To this, I have no definite response. But what I am certain of is we are all innately teachers, and have the ability to contribute, however larger or small, to influence the trajectory of a child. It was the collective effort by the few Black males in my life who worked together to save one Black male from darkness.

---

[4] Kids Count Data Center, A product of The Annie E. Casey Foundation

You could visit countless elementary schools and not find a single Black male teacher or mentor in the classroom, or even in the school building. While Blacks make up 7% of teachers in public education, only 2% are Black males.

We need more Black men to demonstrate manhood and fatherhood. We need more Black men to reaffirm the beauty of our young ladies so they do not have to seek love and validation through the strangeness of another male figure. We need to educate and mentor, but we can only do so if we first use our voices to get other men to engage in the educational battle that is happening in our schools, as Black men are now missing in action.

At the tender age of twelve, I realized I was missing something: a positive Black male presence. I knew my mother had taught me everything she knew at that point. But she could not teach me how to be a Black man in America. I needed a Black man to show me how to deal with the pressures of society and how to navigate them. Upon that realization, I made a life-changing decision. I moved out of my mother's house and into my uncle's house, a Black, middle-aged man, father, husband, police officer, and contributing citizen. This was a bold choice at such a young age, but I truly desired to make something of myself. It was there in my aunt and uncle's home that I saw the reflection of myself that I so desperately wanted. It was in this home that I understood the need and purpose for the

Black male. Frankly, there were just some things that a woman would never be able to teach me. My aunt and uncle provided a more stable environment where I didn't have to focus on my next meal, the shootings in my neighborhood, or trying to do my homework with no heat, or by candle light. I finally lived in an environment that was conducive to my love for school and learning. We all have a chance to make an impact and to strengthen the communities in which our kids are educated. But to make this happen, Black men will have to step up to the plate.

My narrative is just one story. There are countless other stories to illustrate the conditions young Black boys and girls grow up in every day. We must change the narrative so that this cycle does not repeat itself. How? Simply by taking the first step. If we all take a step together, powerful things can happen in our system. Lives can be changed, kids can be saved, and ultimately, communities can begin to flourish once again.

CHAPTER 6
Real Men Raise Other Men

I am not tragically colored. There is no great sorrow dammed up in my soul, nor lurking behind my eyes.... Even in the helter-skelter skirmish that is my life, I have seen that the world is too strong regardless of a little pigmentation more or less.

No, I do not weep at the world—I am too busy sharpening my oyster knife.

—Zora Neale Hurston

Zora Neale Hurston, one of my favorite authors, was introduced to me in middle school through her novel, *Their Eyes Were Watching God*. Another of her pieces resonates with me in the context of the educational landscape, which was underscored through my participation in Teach For

America. Hurston's infamous article, "How It Feels to Be Colored Me," explores how she learns to celebrate her identity and self-esteem while she grapples with the dichotomy of who she is and who others want her to become. But in many cases, pride hinders most men, including me.

Initially, I went to college to become an attorney, and then I thought finance was the career for me. And although through my own experiences as a student, I realized that education was my calling, I never wanted to pursue it. I was always told that teaching wasn't for men, and that I would never be able to take care of my family—if I ever chose to have one. Growing up, I never interacted with married couples aside from my uncle and aunt, who helped raise me from the age of thirteen. Despite consistently getting A's and B's, I was never expected to attend college. It was my self-pride that limited me. The reality is that if only I had been exposed to a consistent Black male presence early on, I would have been challenged to deal with my issues. Instead, I allowed them to fester until adulthood, which caused me to second guess my very existence. Pride often keeps us from exploring our full potential, whether it is because of the insecurities within ourselves or the negative perceptions of others. It is only when we have positive role models and mentors that we can address the things that continue to validate our fears.

Without my uncle, I would not have known how to suppress the pride associated with being a naïve thirteen year old. I recall this memory like it happened yesterday. On a really cold December day as I headed to the closest Metro station to my house, I grabbed my skullcap and placed it on my head. As I did this, my uncle asked, "Are you going to wear that outside?" I thought, "Uh, yeah. It's cold!" I saw this skullcap as nothing more than something to combat the brutal weather, but my uncle saw it as being associated with criminal activity. In his defense, he had been a police officer prior to retiring and joining a business. He was uniquely aware of the potential danger that lurked in the streets, given his experiences in law enforcement. I decided that I was not going to take it off; it was just a hat, right? What was the big deal in wearing it, anyway? My defiance angered my uncle as I aggressively approached him to plead my case. After all, I was a teen, and I thought I knew everything. But that quickly changed as my uncle firmly told me, "You may not agree with my approach, but you will accept and respect the expectations of this house. If not, you can grab your things and leave." Whoa! I was thirteen years old. Where was I going to go? Needless to say, this was the first and last time I spoke to my uncle in that manner. This one encounter changed my life because outside of my brothers, my uncle was the only adult male who served in an authoritative role in my life aside from my two elementary teachers. I loved and respected my mom as a child, but when I looked in the mirror, her image did not reflect back to me, and therefore did not see her as an ultimate authority. Now, I am aware of the controversial nature of this statement. I am married to a strong Black woman who believes in and demonstrates the authority, strength, and courage of a woman each and every day. But in the spirit of radical honesty, as a young Black male, you honor the authority of your father or another Black male differently than you do the authority of your mother or another Black woman. I only had two teachers with whom I would define as being ultimate authority figures in my life. Many of our children, particularly Black males, do not know how to approach someone in ultimate authority simply because they did not experience it growing up. To honor ultimate authority is a learned behavior. This was my challenge.

According to Urie Broffenbrenner's initial Ecological Systems Theory, he suggests that in order to fully understand human development, one must take into account the entire ecological system in which growth occurs. Individuals are shaped by their internal beliefs, family and friends, organizational structures, their neighborhood and community, and societal systems. I would argue that the two most significant components of the social ecological model are: one's internal belief and mindset, and personal relationships with others like parents, teachers, or mentors. If you never understand who you are, you will always be subject to others defining it for you. As Black males, this is often our struggle, especially in education. We are told to fit into a box or ideology that does not mirror how we see ourselves. This is why we are in dire need of Black males in our schools.

Due to labels generally associated with the field of education, men, particularly Black men, do not want to be a part of a system that does not validate their existence. Our students are longing for more than just a face in the classroom. They need a relationship that shows them how to become strong men, and ultimate authority figures. We can discuss why the problem exists, but if we never offer solutions, we are merely rearranging Jenga pieces and expecting the tower to stand firm.

Unopened Books

CHAPTER 7
The Five Black Male Deterrents In Education

As a nation, I believe many of us realize the critical need for more men of color to enter the classroom as teachers or the school building as leaders, but there are unspoken reasons why ninety-eight percent of Black males are opting out of education to pursue other career pathways. I believe these reasons are rooted in what I am calling *The Five Black Male Deterrents To Education.*

The reality is that all professions have both positive and negative aspects. While the field of education, for some, is a third, fourth, or fifth contingency plan, education offers a diverse set of opportunities to develop and advance professionally contrary to what many believe. If we always view education in an undesirable way, we will never appreciate the good that exists within the field. Before I begin, I ask that you remove any blinders, mental models, or barriers about the field of education, and to try to experience the profession with a new, clean perspective. Education is one of the rare fields in which your impact is far greater than you could ever imagine. Think about your favorite teacher. What you remember most, perhaps, is not the lessons he or she taught, but the way he or she made you feel or believe about yourself.

This book suggests an answer to the question: why are men of color reluctant to pursue education as a profession? I believe the answer is associated with social, emotional, financial, and cultural barriers. One or more of these barriers tend to resonate with Black men such that alternative, more attractive, or acceptable professional pathways win out ninety-eight percent of the time.

The Five Black Male Deterrents In Education:

(1) Lack Of Respect In The Field

(2) Limited Opportunities To Advance

(3) Diminution Of Financial Sustainability

(4) Typecasting Black Males

(5) Demanding Workloads

Lack of Respect in the Field

Albert Einstein once said, "I speak to everyone in the same way, whether he is the garbage man or the president of the university." That is true respect. However, in a society where respect and dignity among Black men are challenged daily, one would work hard as hell to protect it and by any means necessary. Money, power, and respect are all interconnected. However, in conversations with other Black men over the years, respect is the number one point of contention that seems to always surface. One friend asked me, "Jermaine, would you rather have your daughter marry a teacher or doctor?" I said, "doctor." He then said, "Jermaine, that is my point!" I acknowledged his point but went on to provide a rationale for my response. I shared with him that I chose the education profession. It was and is still a complicated decision to own and road to travel. I lost respect from some friends and even family members when I told them that I turned down four job offers in the business field to join Teach For America. Folks thought I had lost my whole mind. I heard, "why would you throw your life away, college degree, and endless opportunities for a teaching position?" It was a rough time for me. I felt as though I had to prove myself and validate my choice to pursue education. I felt that I had to show others that it was the right choice for me. It was my purpose, and it should be respected. But again, it is not easy, and requires great sacrifice along the way. Unfortunately, knowing what I do about the life of an educator, a doctor sounded much less knotty.

Our society's perspective on education tends to be fatalistic, cynical, and a system that can never seem to find the Northstar. If you look at countries like China, Singapore, and Korea, the level of respect for teachers is among the highest in the world. Teachers have the same status as doctors. So, what is so different about the United States of America? This is just intolerable and wildly unfortunate for our children who have a constitutional right to a quality education and teaching workforce. The people who spend the most time with our children receive so little respect and compensation. Former Education Minister Lord Adonis said it best: "To recruit the brightest and best, teaching needs to be a high-status occupation."

So why are teachers respected so little? For starters, education was and is dominated by women who were thought to be "better with children". According to the National Center for Education Statistics, in the fall of 2013, there were 3.5 million full-time equivalent elementary and secondary school teachers. Of these, an overwhelming 76 percent of public school teachers were female.[5] I am a strong proponent of female teachers; in fact, some of my best teachers are women. However, the conversations that I have with Black men usually revolve around the lack of

---

[5] National Center for Education Statistics, "Teacher trends," *NCES Fast Facts,* 2016, 2 Feb., 2017 <http://nces.ed.gov/fastfacts/display.asp?id=28>

respect from those outside the educational sector, who often minimize it as a female-only, low-impact, and business-acumen-lacking profession. Black men are not going for that.

<u>Limited Opportunities To Advance</u>

Since entering the education field as a Teach For America corps member in 2010, my primary goal was to become a school principal. For many Black males in education, we commonly share this goal. For me, it was a goal that seemed so out of reach because, quite simply, I did not see or know many Black male principals. In fact, according to the 2016 U.S. Department of Education report on diversity among educators, only about 10 percent of public school principals are black. After years in the field and further consideration, I concluded that my goal was too shortsighted. I shifted my goal to open a network of boarding schools, become Superintendent, and someday become the US Secretary of Education. However, this is a potential pathway that many Black males do not believe is available to them. The daunting truth is that most are stuck in teaching with no clear path up. Why is that so? Is it because they don't have the educational credentials? Or maybe they do not have the leadership skills? Maybe there are better candidates for those roles? I would suggest the answer to those questions is no. Multiple studies have noted the benefits for black students with the same-race teacher, including but not limited, to higher graduation rates.

The limited number of Black males in leadership roles is partly due to the limited number of Black male teachers in the workforce. With such a small pool of candidates how would we ever have more Black males serving in leadership positions? It would be extremely difficult, virtually impossible to do. This underscores the need for more Black men to join the teaching workforce. If we multiply the number of Black male teachers, it could dramatically increase the candidate pool and, as a result, the number of Black males serving in leadership positions; increasing their professional esteem, marketability, and earning potential.

Diminution Of Financial Sustainability

As a man of faith, I believe that a man should first provide for his family spiritually and financially. My mother always told me, "I want you to do better and be better than me" so that you can provide for your family. This is something that many children, particularly children growing up in poverty, hear from their parents. Over time, the pressure or obligation to be able to financially provide for your family gets etched in your psyche, especially as a young Black male. A U.S. Bureau of Labor Statistics (BLS) report noted that the median annual salary for high school teachers was

$56,031 in 2014, while approximately ten percent of teachers serving in limited leadership roles and/or inner-city schools averaged approximately $88,910 per year. There are opportunities in education that offer family sustaining wages, but are largely driven by experience and education, geography, opportunity, and the belief and support of others.

In 2010, I graduated college and headed to Detroit, MI to make a difference, to become a teacher. I had very limited financial support from my family and had to provide for myself. I remember signing my offer letter for an annual salary of $28,000. I brought nearly $800 home every two weeks. I vividly recall how difficult it was to make ends meet to pay rent, buy groceries, clothing, and other expenses. I had to sacrifice all that I had to just survive. I had no funds to purchase furniture and literally slept on an air mattress for half of the school year. I would iron my work clothes on a sheet placed on the floor and ate hotdogs and beans three to four times a week. I would go into department stores and window shop for all of the things I wanted but could not afford. Friends would call and ask how things were going and to keep from breaking down, I would dishonestly say, "Things are great, I am enjoying my experience and growing as a person". When friends or colleagues wanted to take trips or go on vacations, I would say that I had to work. Times were very hard but I persisted and maintained my commitment and drive to make a difference for my students. I would take the little money that I had to buy breakfast bars for my students because they would often come to school hungry and lacked energy to focus on solving basic math problems. I purchased books, pencils, tissue and other materials to ensure my students had what they needed. I recall being stuck on the side of the road several times because I did not have enough gas money to get to and from school. This was reality for me early on in my educational career. In all honesty, it was not what I thought I was signing up for.

Several people tried to convince me that I needed to find a new career. In truth, I gave it some thought. More than once. Over and over again I asked myself why I was doing what I was doing. But then realized, if not me, then who would cultivate the young males and females who occupy the seats in our school buildings? It was a difficult conclusion to reach but an internal nudging, or perhaps nagging, convinced me that education was my purpose. It was sobering.

Typecasting Black Males

A persistent myth is that Black men are best suited for, or most effective in disciplinary roles. Now, let's address the elephant in the room by calling out why that tends to be the go-to role for far too many Black men. The male presence, particularly Black male presence, often connotes authority, protection, or fear in some instances but that is another topic for another book. Because of that, Black men have often been tagged as the person who can more effectively manage behavioral issues, in-school suspensions, school culture, or dean of student roles which is all code for behavior management. Though, I will acknowledge that Black men who serve in these kind of roles is beneficial to children who frequently find themselves in disciplinary-related predicaments. A Black male presence can mitigate escalations that typically lead to short or long-term suspensions, meltdowns, or physical altercations.

Most people who look at education through an external lens have a distorted view of it. They consider the drawbacks of the field, and find it challenging to acknowledge or even embrace the good. My students saying, "Hello" and "How are you doing, Mr. Gassaway?" is the motivation that reaffirms my daily decision to stay committed to education. While I have often been typecast at various schools, I hear those gentle voices of my students. It is not easy, but these subtle reminders keep me from giving up when some would consider it to be excusable. Having the role of the person who can best manage a classroom is very difficult and sometimes draining. However, I have made it a priority to become an instructional leader for this very same reason. I passed up numerous opportunities to become a Dean of Culture because it is the typical role people within the educational field believe is suited for a Black male.

No one understands the complexities of this field like an educator. It is often stated that to change the system, you must first be a part of it. When I mention that I am a teacher, I get cynical responses like, "Oh, that's good," or "that is such a noble profession", or "Kids are so bad now. I feel sorry for you." It is a tough profession. I get it. But I love my job. I recognize that I have a purpose, and that some do not share that same passion. Taking on roles that are primarily behavior management focused is not a complete waste of time or unneeded; however, it can hinder the retention of Black males particularly those who have felt typecast.

<u>Demanding Workloads</u>

Teaching is not easy, but it is worth it. On the one hand, my experience with Teach For America provided real-time, classroom support to ensure that my students were academically successful. On the other hand, my first placement school could have cared less about my professional development and, to some extent, the students. It was my TFA program director who spent a significant amount of time helping me write lesson plans, create rigorous assessments, strengthen my classroom management skills, and analyze my students' data. As my life started to transition from bachelorhood to being a married man with a family, the workload became even more challenging. When I was single, I did not mind working countless hours to master best practices to become the most effective teacher possible. I would often stay up until twelve or one o'clock in the morning grading papers, working on lesson plans, creating PowerPoint presentations, and the list could go on. Now, as a husband and father, I am still committed to working hard, but I also enjoy spending time with my family. I look forward to reading with my daughter or sitting down to enjoy dinner without thinking about work. Working these kind of hours has never been an issue but as you get older and your lifestyle and family structure changes, it requires a self-assessment of your approach to work-life balance. In some other fields like doctors, lawyers, dentists, or entrepreneurs, the tradeoff is financial compensation for long hours. You work hard, and get appropriately compensated for your time and hard work.

The Five Deterrents have caused many Black men to flee from the fight for educational equity. It is deeply rooted in societal, cultural, and financial structures that present this profession as less than desirable. To many, the juice is simply not worth the squeeze. However, through my experiences as a conscious educator over the years, I feel confident that we will yield the same results in education if we, as Black men, continue to wait on the sidelines, silently validating the persistence of unopened books. I believe Mahatma Gandhi said it best: “We must be the change we wish to see in the world.” Our world. Our neighborhoods. Our families. I give everything that I have to ensure future generations see themselves when they see me.

CHAPTER 8
A Call to the Economically Disadvantaged

> We have come over a way that with tears has been watered, We have come, treading our path through the blood of the slaughtered.
>
> —James Weldon Johnson

Exposure

As a kid, I idolized Black athletes and Dr. Martin Luther King, Jr. These were the larger than life, influential Black men that I looked up to. As a Black man, I will not say that there are no great Black men in this world, that would be totally egregious, but my question is: Why were they so rare in my world as a kid? This question illustrates the physical and emotional deprivation growing up.

As a classroom instructor, I taught students who made significant academic gains, exceeded standardized test scores, and received high school credit before they even walked through the doors of a high school. I instilled within each of them a sense of belonging in a world that often says that they are not worthy of much. But that was not enough. The battle that our students are fighting is so much larger than education; the chaos starts outside but seamlessly finds its way to the classroom. Many schools attempt to barricade the chaos but if we cannot effectively provide the support and resources to help them combat the evils of their reality, we have failed, and failed terribly. Thus, we must fight together in all areas of education, from classrooms to boardrooms, from practice fields to practice labs, from church halls to juvenile detention centers.

My entire life changed, all because people cared, and dared to do more than what was required. Had it not been for my sixth-grade teacher, who told me about an opportunity to attend boarding school; or my high school coach in boarding school, who instilled a sense of integrity and hard work; or my uncle, and church mentor who taught me about being a Black man in America, I don't know where I would be. If not for my former superintendent, who recognized my potential as a classroom teacher and promoted me to school-wide leadership, I don't know if I would be writing this book right now. The commonality among each of these experiences is that someone believed in me when I did not have enough strength to believe in myself. Education is a collective effort. This is why the need is great for Black men – they are the missing link. Our students are books and unless we have people who are able to turn their delicate pages, we will continue to talk about achievement and opportunity gaps, increases in incarceration rates, and the reality of kids from low-income communities not being realized.

Black men can offer a diverse set of experiences to expose students to careers and fields that they have never heard of. Ideally, kids need to see people who have been successful, and people who can share their values and beliefs. We must knock on doors, schools, community and civic centers, libraries, churches, and anywhere else to get involved and influence the lives of children who need it the most. In the schools where I have worked, not once did I witness professionals knock on our door and ask for opportunities to serve our kids. Our kids need you as a teacher, mentor, or sponsor. Remember, we are all teachers who have a responsibility to serve, educate, and mentor future generations.

As teachers, we offer our students unique perspectives and experiences; we become the reflection that they seek to embody. The truth is that if we do nothing, we are just as guilty as the person who attempted something, but failed miserably. Since we are the people they see daily, we have the perfect opportunity to change their paradigm. The statistics are just as startling as they were decades ago. Incarceration rates are still on the rise. And if we are not intentionally fighting it, kids from low-income communities will continue to fill those prison cells.

But mentorship alone is not enough. We need sponsorships. W. E. B. Du Bois, in his book, *The Black Reconstruction in America,* said, "[T]he slave went free; stood a brief moment in the sun; then moved back again toward slavery." We must be a constant voice for our students that not only affirms them, but also shows them how to become greater than the generations before. We need them to be great, and they need us to take a stand. Who will be the ones to stand in the gap?

Access

Another way we can help turn the pages of our kids is through access. Access is defined as "the right or privilege to approach, reach, enter, or make use of something." It is the factor that is often missing in addressing educational equality. As a teacher or mentor, your role is to be the bridge—to research opportunities and to expose students to an endless buffet of opportunities. Children from low-income backgrounds have far fewer opportunities to interface with people whose role is to be the bridge. We should all know this well by now, but if a privileged child seeks an internship, she can simply ask her parent to call their buddy and make the connection. On the flip side, if a less fortunate child seeks an internship, she will jump through many hoops to simply get on the right path to get connected with someone who can point her in the right direction. On one side, you have clear access to internships, academic enrichment, influence, and guidance. And on the other, limited resources, influence, and guidance, if any at all. It is a never-ending cycle. If a privileged child struggles with the ACT or SAT, their parents can study with them, or afford to provide the necessary tutoring or test prep. If their child wants to pick up a new skill like skating, swimming, or playing the piano, they can arrange for that to happen. That is access at its core. Ultimately, this is the difference maker for our kids.

I am by no means suggesting that kids with limited or no access cannot become successful, because they absolutely can. I am a living, breathing, walking, talking example of it. However, the road to success with limited or no access may look much different, but they are navigable. It simply requires a little more work, belief, and commitment. Often in low-income communities, we miss connections, or perhaps do not know where to find them. If someone has already mastered what you are currently doing, why would you seek to do it alone? This is the difference between mentorship and sponsorship. You cannot have one without the other. We need more Black men to not just mentor our students, but to sponsor. Kids usually have an idea where they want to go, but do not know the how to get there. At fifteen, I knew I wanted to attend a school that was academically rigorous and would prepare me for college, a good career, and life. But realizing that I was not doing well in school, and, quite frankly, not attending a school that could put me on a path to success, I wrote a letter to the Board of Education to transfer to a different school – I was denied. Access was barred simply because I did not have good grades and my zip code. But I knew there was more in store for me beyond my current circumstance. The idea of "more" caused me to strive harder than ever before.

CHAPTER 9
Closed Doors

> Where justice is denied, where poverty is enforced, where ignorance prevails, and where any one class is made to feel that society is in an organized conspiracy to oppress, rob, and degrade them, neither persons nor property will be safe.
>
> —Frederick Douglass

Imagine a young, academically struggling, Black boy from the toughest parts of DC writing to the DC Board of Education to transfer schools because he felt unsafe, and hated school because of the chaos that he experienced while there. That was me. I saw a need, and I wanted it fixed. Although their response was not what I had hoped for – I was denied twice – it fueled my passion for education and caused me to reflect on my ability to influence. As educators, we are sometimes afraid to speak out because we spend time weighing the costs. Think of it like this, if you were working in corporate America and you knew that your employer's policies were illegal, would you speak up? You probably would not. Your first thought might be, "I may lose my job." But as educators, we have to be willing to sacrifice our own comfort and convenience for the sake of something far greater.

In 2002, I attended a low-performing high school in a suburb of Maryland. I witnessed gambling in the classrooms, inconsiderate teachers, teachers afraid of students, inadequate resources, chaos, and confusion; it was safe to say that the classroom was no longer a place where learning was valued. For me, it became a threat to achieving my long-term goals. I wanted out. But over time, I thought that if no one else valued my education or saw me as an important and valuable person, then why should I? I became resistant to the concept of learning, often skipping class or not attending school altogether. As would be expected, my grades dropped. In my frustration, without any parental support, I decided to write to the Board of Education to request a school transfer. I was a fifteen-year-at the time. I thought that if no one else would, I would take a stand. As I opened the letter from the Board, I read two words: "Request denied." I appealed. Those same words headlined the first sentence. I was devastated.

Midway through the tenth grade, I reached out to my former sixth-grade teacher, who told me about an opportunity to attend a boarding school. The school, Piney Woods School, was 600 miles away from home in Pineywoods, Mississippi. In 2003, I applied and was accepted. The decision was simple – I am leaving. I attended Piney Woods during my junior and senior year of high school. My mentor, Tim States, helped raise money to ensure that I had the basic necessities. I later received a financial need scholarship to cover additional costs to live. He also drove me sixteen hours from Washington, DC to Pineywoods, MS in Fall 2004. It was a culture shock. There were students from France, Ethiopia, Cameroon, and all fifty states. I had never been outside of the D.C. area. It was a bold move, and ultimately, a life-changing one.

I did not realize it at the time but writing to the DC Board of Education planted a seed that would one day bring me back to the field of education. A question I often ask myself is, "Why did it take this experience to get me to care about education in this country?" Local boards of education serve an important role in the American education system. Whether they are elected or appointed, board members serve within their communities in several vital ways:

- First and most importantly, the school board advocates for the interests of the students that it serves. Unlike many businesses or government agencies, school boards focus primarily on the state and quality of education.

- When it comes to making major decisions about school programs, these boards use their reasonable judgment to incorporate their beliefs about what students should know and be able to do.

- School boards should be easily accessible to the public and should be held accountable for the schools in their communities.

- School boards act as community overseers, ensuring tax dollars are being used to give their students a quality education. If possible, this should include the chance to make an informed decision about pursuing higher education.

This is the textbook purpose of a board of education. However, we must ask ourselves: if the purpose of the board of education is to serve the community, why is the community not serving on the board? At some point, we must take ownership of our actions and show up for our children in ways that, for many of us, others failed to show up for us.

School boards tend to consist of business leaders and government officials, who are disconnected from the classroom. We need individuals who witness the dynamics of teaching and learning daily to articulate the real issues and opportunities. We need parents, teachers, community-based organizations and partners. We need more Black males sitting on school boards to make decisions that will positively affect future generations. Consider this, when was the last time you actually watched a school board meeting on television? When was the last time you went to one in person? Some of us, perhaps, have never been. We cannot effect change from comfortable seats or from disgruntled conversations with coworkers. We must be active advocates for the sake of our kids, for the sake of this nation, and ultimately, for the sake of ourselves. History has taught us that it is bound to repeat itself; thus, what we ignore now will affect us later.

I can petition the school board and lay claim to the issues that exist, but if no one joins me, louder choruses silence my voice. I need you to help fill in the gap. There are places that my voice cannot carry me, but when joined together, we can create an uproar that transcends communities, policies, practices, and structures. The next time you find yourself complaining about the issues within the educational system, ask yourself this question: How am I contributing to or combating the issue? Your Voice. Our Vote. Be the advocates we so urgently need.

CHAPTER 10
Diversify Quickly

> I am an invisible man. I am a man of substance, of flesh and bone, fiber and liquids—and I might even be said to possess a mind. I am invisible, understand, simply because people refuse to see me.
>
> —Ralph Ellison

There are more than 16 million children growing up in poverty in the United States. Of those 16 million, one in three will not graduate from high school. And only 18% will enroll in a four-year college. Of those enrolled, only 9% will receive a bachelor's degree by the age of twenty-five. As I pondered these numbers and what they meant for our students, I realized that at some point in time, I was included in those statistics. I was part of the statistics that boldly rips children from their vision of success. I was part of the statistics that sought to destroy a generation of people, all because the education system was deemed broken. Others placed me in this group simply due to my geographical location.

I was fortunate enough to have teachers and mentors along the way who believed in my potential and helped me achieve my goals. But while I may not be a part of these statistics anymore, I am forever connected to the truth that lies beneath these numbers. My nieces and nephews, who currently live in DC's Ward 8 community, are connected to these numbers. These statistics represent the inequalities in our education system, not in our kids. They represent the need for a common effort by all to equip our children with the tools and resources they need to access the expansive world of learning so that they, too, can become productive citizens in our society, not just statistics in our criminal justice system. We all understand the direct correlation between the lack of education and criminality. In fact, the United States imprisons a larger percentage of its Black population than South Africa did at the height of the Apartheid. In our nation's capital, it is estimated that three out of four young Black men (and nearly all of those in the poorest neighborhoods) can expect to serve time in prison. These statistics suggest that far too many people could care less about the outcomes of kids growing up in low-income communities.

The fact is that more than half of all public school students are children of color. Surprisingly, the same does not apply to the ones who are teaching them. Latino, Black, Asian, and Native American teachers account for only 17% of public school instructors. Although only 2% of educators in the United States are Black, it doesn't have to be that way. I can unapologetically say that education is one of the best decisions I have ever made. Every day, I witness the lack of racial diversity in the school system. However, I can also stand in front of my students to impart knowledge and help them make informed decisions. Teach For America gave me a clear purpose and represented what I wanted to see in the classroom. Just over a short period of time as a corps member and alumnus, I have seen the organization's vast progress and its commitment to diversifying the classroom—one teacher at a time. I have watched as Teach For America has led the way in recruiting more Black male teachers. The organization works with various organizations; it does not just talk about the 2%, but is instrumental in increasing it. The work it does is truly commendable. They have become a voice in the educational landscape:

- 47% of its teachers come from low-income backgrounds.
- 49% of Teach For America corps members

identify as people of color.

- Four out of five Teach For America alumni work in education or within low-income communities.
- 86% of principals say they would hire a corps member again.
- Nine in ten principals are satisfied with Teach For America's support of corps members.

With statistics like these, the scope of this organization's influence is undeniable. We need more Teach For America like organizations in education, but it will not happen unless we act, demand change, and begin to view other teachers and ourselves as diverse individuals who can impart knowledge in the classroom. Furthermore, and most importantly, we can be the image for kids to relate to and reinforce the right to dream and achieve. Children need to see Black male teachers and mentors in their schools to unmask the preconceptions of their own cultural identity. There are many ways we can think about diversity and its meanings. Diversity, according to the *Merriam-Webster Dictionary*, is the "quality or state of having many different forms, types, and ideas, or the state of having people who are [of] different races or who [are of] different cultures in a group or organization." Growing up in the inner city of Washington, DC, the educational landscape looked much different in the '90s than it does now. I can vividly remember the immediate identification when I met my second-grade teacher, a Black male. I had never encountered a Black male educator before and it was not an image that I was accustomed to. At the time, I was not used to the mere presence of an intelligent Black man; thus, my level of interest was heightened.

Thinking back to kindergarten and first grade, I had mostly Black female teachers who were equally phenomenal. However, I was just not invested. Most of the time, I would get in trouble. I rarely did my work. By the second grade, I was already one or two grade levels behind in both reading and math. But grade three was different. There was something about the presence of my Black male teacher that caused something to shift. For reasons unknown to me at the time, I would envision myself as this person. No matter what the lesson was about, I would instantly take on his persona; I completed classroom tasks and homework assignments much more frequently. I was simply more engaged. He had my attention, and I was at his disposal. For me, he represented what I wanted to become—a successful Black man. It was this connection that inspired me to be like him; thus, in everything I did, I mirrored his presence. I longed to be him.

Perhaps the distinction between my Black female teachers and my Black male teacher is this: he represented something that was rare, almost like a delicacy in education. I saw my Black female teachers as motherly figures; because they reminded me of a motherly figure and I was more inclined to dismiss them. I was not obsessed with their presence, nor did they intrigue me. I had a mother. But I did not have a father. That is not to say that I did this intentionally or that my relationship with my mother was flawed, but I truly believe that how we relate to our parents is mirrored within the classroom. Students who lack consistently involved fathers often express combative or violent behavior towards other men, which is usually associated with the denial of an authority figure. I say this not to suggest that I had "mommy" or "daddy" issues, but to note that these are real challenges that exist within communities across America, not just within Black households.

It was his mere presence that made me rise to the challenge because I did not want to fail him. He believed in me, and I believed in his teaching. He made a connection with me and I was able to see myself when I saw him. That was the clear distinction for me. This is the added benefit of the Black male educator, especially in elementary school. Fast forward to my experience as a fourth-grade teacher. It was like déjà vu to witness my students imitating me. In both experiences, there is a commonality: a Black male. Schools today lack the diversity that is needed to afford students a holistic education that supports and prepares them for the real world. I had a great second-grade teacher, but the reality is that some students will unfortunately never get to experience something similar.

When I think about the schools I have been a part of, and the leadership teams I have worked with over the span of my teaching career, I am reminded of the value of collaboration with others from diverse backgrounds. When these discussions are held, I am often saddened by the fact that I am the only Black male in the room. I have seen this scenario play out time and time again, and I am always left with the same question: Why? This usually leads to other questions like: Why do I have to be the one to represent an entire culture? Why am I the only one here? Where are the rest of us? Then, I am left wondering: How did we, as a nation, get to the point where the Black male has been distanced from the classroom and the education sector as a whole?

Questions like these spark my spirit of advocacy. Why is it that we have diversity initiatives in the workplace, but much less so in education? True education can only arise through dialogue among a diverse group of people. Without many voices, we will forever be elevating one voice and minimizing others, whether intentionally or unintentionally. As a nation, we must call everyone to the decision-making table to initiate change within America's public school system.

CHAPTER 11
Call to Action

The writer cannot expect to be excused from the task of reeducation and regeneration that must be done. In fact, he should march right in front.

—Chinua Achebe

According to the *Merriam-Webster Dictionary, action* is defined as the "initiation by which one demands or enforces one's rights; the bringing about of an alteration by force or through a natural agency; an act of will." The term implies a cause-and-effect relationship, that is, something must take place for something else to occur.

Perhaps you've read this entire book and you are still unsure of your role in education. However, it is my hope that you conceptualize the dire need for your presence as a

Black male on a daily or weekly basis. Your voice is more powerful than you ever may know. Therefore, I issue this call to action.

The Call to Action

The doorbell is ringing. Will you answer, Black men? Will you answer, faith-based communities? Will you answer, business owners? Will you answer, educational leaders? How will you respond?

To Our Black Men

When you think of the Black male, a few words should come to mind. Words like powerful, bold, and resilient. Our kids need to feel the warmth of your presence, the wave of your confidence, and the calmness of your speech. Our students need to know that you care, and that you are not just a ghostly figure who flits in and out of their lives. They need to know that you are real and valued because they, too, are like you.

It is not often that you, as a Black male, feel valued in society, but in this particular field, you are a valued asset. It is sad that you are considered an anomaly rather than the standard. The 2% often carry the weight of your daily absence, but the reality is that this is getting harder. I urge you to use your voice to demand your place within education—to show America that we are more than how we are defined.

You do not have to be a teacher, but can serve as a mentor or in any other educational capacity. It is time that we take off our blinders about the term "teacher." We are all teachers, and it is our responsibility to do our part. I am reminded of the question that is often asked when people refuse to create change: If not you, then who? Who will be the one to close the achievement gap for students of color? Who will reaffirm the identities of our future astronauts, doctors, lawyers, entrepreneurs, and teachers? The answer has to be **YOU**. No one else can stand for you, but we can stand collectively, hand in hand, to affect policies to change the legislative and educational landscape of America.

It is time that we begin to envision the life that we desire for the heirs of our legacy. It is time that we stop being silent and start being audible. We need your intelligence, ingenuity, and influence.

Black men, our children and communities need you. We need you to join this war in education by being a presence in the classroom and a voice in the community. We need you to take your rightful place as men to change the trajectory of our kids.

We need you. For there is no us without you.

To Our Parents

Before your kids ever enter the classroom, you are the first person they see. You are the breath that maintains their heartbeat. You are the true model of their existence. You are the one that they yearn for in the middle of the night. You are the first one who comes to their defense. You are the depositor of knowledge, morality instructor, and encouragement provider. You are their first teacher.

Far too often, our kids experience your lack of presence within education because you simply trust that they can do it alone. But they cannot. No matter how old they grow or how fast they mature, they will always need you to guide them. Even in adulthood, the presence of a mother and a father cannot easily be replaced. Your contribution is equally as vital as that of the Black male educator, for we need you to teach our sons and daughters how to become young men and young women.

We need you to advocate—no, we really need you to break through the barred doors of the school, and be the leader in the school building. We need you to serve on parent-teacher organizations (PTOs). We need you to get involved so you can help the next generation of parents. We need you to be the bridge between access and opportunity.

You are important to our success; without you, we would not exist. I urge you to remain committed to the educational journey in spite of the challenges you may face.

Be the voice that demands change.

To Our Faith-Based Organizations

In the early establishment of the church, it was called the *ekklēsía,* which translates from Greek as "out from and to." As sons and daughters of religious faith, we are called to partake in *koinonia*; in Greek, the term means "community; communion," or a coming together of a group of believers. Thus, the historic church represented a body of people who were not confined to a particular location; wherever the believers gathered was considered to be the church. It was the establishment of the people that defined it as a church, not the establishment itself.

Your presence alone is the church. You are walking believers of the faith that you subscribe to. To convince the nations, you are called to be witnesses to and examples of your religion. James 2:26 states, "faith without works is dead"; therefore, if we only seek God through prayer, but do not follow his instructions or act on our beliefs, we become crippled in our faith.

As a leader, church member, or representative of the community, your voice is powerful beyond measure because you are the connection that prompts others to act. Historically, faith-based organizations have been instrumental in galvanizing groups of people to partake in political action to strengthen communities by mandating change. Pastors or religious leaders are often considered the very fabric of our communities because they represent the voice of the people.

As a faith-based organization and as a religious leader, you are seen as a teacher. We need you to develop and mentor leaders in the church to revitalize the state of education. Make it a priority in your community and in your church to be the activists who change the educational framework.

From the pulpit to the boardroom, we need you to push the conversation forward. We need you to be aware of the 2%.

We solicit your prayers and we invite you to act.

To Our Business Owners

You supply the jobs, and as educational institutions, we supply the candidates to fill them. But if students are not adequately trained within the classroom, their lack of skill is transferred to the job sector, creating problems for both employers and employees and reducing efficiency within the workplace. Achieve, a nonprofit organization focused on college and career readiness efforts, reported:

> In 2005, as many as 40 percent of the nation's high school graduates say they are inadequately prepared to deal with the demands of employment and postsecondary education, putting their own individual success and the nation's economic growth in peril, according to a national survey of 2,200 Americans, including nearly 1,500 recent high school graduates, 400 employers and 300 college instructors.

Even ten years later, various news outlets have validated these findings, suggesting that the data has not changed. Research shows that a gap exists between work habits and students' inability to read and understand complex texts associated with math, science, and writing. Students' unpreparedness for the workforce is not a new phenomenon; for centuries, schools and business owners have sought to devise new approaches to education through established partnerships. Although employers have seen great growth in workforce programs, there are still some inconsistencies between the classroom and the job sector.

Our kids are no longer competing within the United States, but globally. Thus, for us to maintain our status as a nation, we must make sure we not only educate our students, but also equip them with diverse skill sets. We need innovative leaders, critical thinkers, and inventive problem solvers within the job sector. This will have a huge economic impact. For the sake of our communities and for the sake of America, let's put our students to work by giving them adequate training.

I urge you to become more concerned about the state of our nation than your bottom line. I urge you to evaluate your policies to ensure that your company is diverse in nature, and offer opportunities for employees to volunteer, mentor, offer job-shadowing opportunities, or sponsor a child. It matters. Education is a vital part of what makes American society work. If we do not have a workforce that can meet the growing demands of global industry, we are doing our students a disservice.

Find your place within the education system to effect lasting change.

To Our Educational Leaders

You are the core of education; without your drive for equity, we would be worse off than we are now. For your decisive stance on all things education, we thank you.

We understand the pressures associated with your position. We have read the various reports and policies surrounding the plight of education. The data continue to reiterate the same concerns, yet the state of education remains dismal in many parts of the country. The lack of progress does not squarely fall on the shoulders of educational leaders but we encourage you to invite diverse teams of teachers to sit at the same decision-making tables so we can work together to creatively solve persistent challenges in education.

I urge you to hold yourselves accountable to diverse teaching staff, and encourage opportunities for Black males to serve as mentors or sponsors to students in your buildings. Diversity is the core of American society. We need different perspectives, cultural experiences, and knowledge to give our students a well-rounded education. We need more than just the 2% of Black male teachers within the classroom; we need mentors, business leaders, and community partners to ensure our educational will one day serve all students well.

We ask that you consult teachers as they know the complexities of the field like the back of their hand. We ask that you allocate resources to schools appropriately. Extend ample opportunities for professional development and give teachers the time to engage and learn within a safe space. Fix our school buildings so we can spend more time learning, and less time focused on managing basic unmet needs.

No longer will we sit quietly waiting on a decision to be made. Instead, we will willfully pursue our desired course of action in pursuit of achieving what is best for children. We will be the vehicles of reform. We are asking that you join forces with us in this endeavor. For we cannot act alone—we need you.

The Call: Will You Answer?

Now that the call has been made, which side of the educational debate will you be on? It is our hope that you will accept this challenge to act, that you will consider the millions of boys and girls who are currently in the classroom, and will remember that they will one day be your sons and daughters or your nieces and nephews. Remember the state of education when you were younger. Remember all of the things that you wish you had been taught or exposed to.

Let this be your drive. Let this compel you to act. Our words are empty if we never produce the appropriate action.

Unopened Books is more than a conversation starter. It seeks to offer the perspective of the 2% and to highlight the need for more Black men within education. This book urges all of us, including myself, to take an introspective look into our lives and to recognize the circle of our influence. And it is not enough for us to recognize it. We must join with others in the educational dialogue occurring all around the world. The goal of this book is to challenge educational leaders, entrepreneurs, teachers, and other stakeholders within education to create diversity, not only on paper, but also in the school building, by inviting business professionals and mentors into the classroom. No longer can we exist separately; we are overdue for an explosion of collaboration and intellectual expression.

As stakeholders in education, we must demand change everywhere; from the White House to our state capitol. We must boisterously express our complaints. We must provide a plan of action for change, for it is not enough for us to demand it without concrete strategies. It is time that we speak up. It is time that we unmute our voices and proclaim the injustices in the system. It is time that we mandate what we have envisioned. Now is the time.

Our lives depend on it. Our future depends on it. Our unopened books depend on it.

Unopened Books

Afterword

Since entering the field of education in the '90s, I have worked with predominantly African-American students. In my roles as a teacher, principal, vice-president of achievement, and chief academic officer, I have traveled across the Midwest to support schools and to raise the capacity of leaders to enhance the success of students on a national and local level. From my observations, I have noticed a common trend: the need for more African-American male role models for our students.

Not only do I know from personal experience, but research also confirms that African-American boys have a greater chance of going to prison than graduating from high school. This was the problem when I became an administrator in Detroit.

In response, New Paradigm for Education (NPFE) was created to develop, expand, and replicate more high-quality, high-performing schools in Detroit—one school at a time. This non-profit organization, which is located, operated, and governed in the city, consists of educators, community advocates, and business leaders who have dedicated years of service to children. New Paradigm for Education prides itself on having an absolute determination to maximize students' learning potential through proven education practices, operating in all phases of school design, planning, and program implementation.

NPFE currently runs five schools in Detroit. The Detroit Edison Public School Academy (hereafter known as DEPSA) opened its doors in September 1998 and is recognized as a national academic leader. DEPSA's nearly 1,000 pre-K through eighth-grade students come from various backgrounds and familial structures. In standardized assessments, DEPSA continuously outperforms the district and the state. Indeed, its reputation draws commuters from Metropolitan Detroit and from the surrounding suburban areas.

Capitalizing on its success, NPFE opened DEPSA Early College of Excellence (ECE) in 2013. It is the highest-performing non-application high school in Detroit, with an ACT average of 19 for all students and 25 for legacy students matriculating from the pre-K–8 flagship. ECE offers innovative, rigorous, and relevant college-prep learning to train students for ongoing achievement, dynamic global leadership, and deep personal fulfillment. We offer ninth–twelfth-grade students the global awareness and higher-order thinking skills that will motivate them to transform Detroit and the state from a manufacturing-based to a knowledge-based economy.

In 2011, Jermaine Gassaway came to DEPSA as an instructor by way of Teach For America. He devoted time to tutor struggling students and participated in academy activities before and after school. Mr. Gassaway was reliable and flexible when completing assigned tasks. Moreover, as a teacher, he used refined and effective instructional practices that enabled his students to learn and process information. Mr. Gassaway built relationships and fostered mutual respect, and his classroom was always active and productive. He persistently encouraged his students to work independently, think critically, and share their ideas. He also chose to pilot a new math program. Finally, his mentorship of male students was a key element in his success as a teacher.

In 2012, Mr. Gassaway transitioned to a curriculum coach position at DEPSA. As well as supporting the staff, he collaborated with other coaches to facilitate data meetings, did after-school tutoring, created district assessments, and graded math homework. Mr. Gassaway also paired with the elementary principal to conduct parent meetings. He continued in his mentorship role by holding individual student conferences during lunch.

Mr. Gassaway set a stellar example for all our students, but especially for our young African-American males. He was a problem solver and goal setter who carried himself with great dignity and integrity—two qualities that need to be on display for our next generation. It is imperative that we continue to funnel talented, committed, and strong African-American male role models into the classroom to ensure that our boys and girls can have one-on-one mentorship opportunities. Students need to see men of color in leadership positions to validate the importance of education. We are fortunate to have a book that addresses the vital role of such African-American male role models in the classroom.

Kimberly Bland
Chief Academic Officer

Words from my Mentor

Jermaine Gassaway is a young man who has confronted many obstacles to emerge as an influential voice in the educational dialogue for years to come. His background and clear vision allow him to navigate the current turbulence in academic circles regarding the education of Black students. Jermaine's humble childhood gives him a unique perspective on the challenges motivating and informing young Black minds today.

Jermaine was born in Washington, D.C. Observing older siblings entrapped in a system designed to stunt intellectual growth while replenishing the prison industrial complex, Jermaine was determined to succeed using any means necessary. Riding public transportation across town to attend church with his grandmother gave him the sense of compassion that is so necessary for sparking young minds.

While sputtering in high school, Jermaine decided to leave the familiarity of the Greater Washington Area, traveling over 600 miles to attend the acclaimed Piney Woods Boarding School in Jackson, Mississippi. Piney Woods provided a stable, disciplined, and academically challenging environment. It fulfilled Jermaine's intellectual curiosity, while instilling in him the importance of leadership and giving back to his community.

After graduating from Piney Woods, Jermaine enrolled at Johnson C. Smith (HBCU), where he held several student body positions that allowed him to interact with most of his peers on campus and learn about their diverse educational backgrounds. These discussions with other Black achievers gave him additional insight into how to motivate young African-American students. Questions about why to pursue higher education, or how college can add value, were answered. These discussions also moved him away from hypothetical situations towards real life.

Taking a position as a teacher in inner-city Detroit was the final step in the real-world transition for Jermaine after graduating from Johnson C. Smith. Daily classroom interactions allowed him to see, hear, and connect with young people who faced obstacles far greater than assignments. If they needed after-school tutoring, Jermaine provided it. If they needed understanding, he understood. If they needed motivation, he motivated. Jermaine's goal has been to empower young Black minds while steering them toward the road to success.

Timothy States
Mentor, and father figure

ABOUT THE AUTHOR

Jermaine is currently the Founding Assistant Principal of Rocketship Rise Academy located in Southeast Washington, DC. Prior to joining the Rocketship network, Jermaine served as a lead teacher at two charter schools in Charlotte, NC. At KIPP Charlotte, he served as the lead 8th grade math teacher where 94% of his students passed the End of Grade assessment which earned them high school credit.

In 2010, Jermaine joined Teach for America, a national non-profit organization that places recent college graduates in the classroom to grow as an influencer in the broader fight for equity and opportunity. He completed the corps in Detroit, MI where he served as a fourth grade teacher at Detroit Edison Public School Academy. In 2012, Jermaine accepted a role as math Curriculum Coordinator, serving over 800 students in grades K-5.

Jermaine aspires to one day found a boarding school in Washington, DC to serve low-income students across the metropolitan area. Jermaine graduated from Johnson C. Smith University with a bachelor's degree in Finance. He is currently pursuing a Masters of Business Administration at The University of North Carolina at Chapel Hill. Jermaine and his wife, Apri, have one daughter named Abigail.

Made in the USA
Middletown, DE
22 May 2018